GROUND

Sturmgeschütz, Vol. 2

Germany's WWII Assault Gun (StuG): The Late War Versions

DAVID DOYLE

4880 Lower Valley Road • Atglen, PA 19310

Other Schiffer Books by the Author:

Panzerkampfwagen IV: The Backbone of Germany's WWII Tank Forces, ISBN: 978-0-7643-5359-8

USS Yorktown (CV-5): From Design and Construction to the Battles of Coral Sea and Midway, ISBN: 978-0-7643-5288-1

M40 Gun Motor Carriage and M43 Howitzer Motor Carriage in WWII and Korea, ISBN: 978-0-7643-5402-1

Library of Congress Control Number: 2017955741

Designed by Justin Watkinson
Type set in Impact/Minion Pro/Univers LT Std

ISBN: 978-0-7643-5538-7
Printed in China

Published by Schiffer Publishing, Ltd.
4880 Lower Valley Road
Atglen, PA 19310
Phone: (610) 593-1777; Fax: (610) 593-2002
E-mail: Info@schifferbooks.com
www.schifferbooks.com

Acknowledgments

Compiling a book of this nature is a task that requires a number of people, sometimes working together, sometimes independently, for a number of years, often spanning decades. Much of this book comprises archival images, with the adjacent photo credits providing a modest background to those images. However, a greater explanation is warranted. The Patton Museum, formerly at Ft. Knox, Kentucky, held two large collections that were used in preparing this book. One of these was assembled by Robert J. Icks over a period of decades. Col. Icks, a career ordnance officer, was also one of the earliest authors of books on military vehicles. The second collection from the Patton Museum that was utilized for this project is the collection of Richard Hunnicutt. Richard, a long-time friend of Walter Spielberger, had copies of much of Walter's collection of materials—so much so that when Walter's home burned, destroying many records, Richard was able to provide the copies that were the basis for rebuilding the collection. Richard connected me to Walter, and both were gracious in assisting me with assembling my own collection.

Perhaps even more convoluted is the story of many of the images in this volume that were sourced from the US National Archives and Records Administration. This agency is the official custodian of US military-created photographs of the World War II era. However, beyond that, the archives also held the German wartime photograph collection now held by the Bundesarchiv in Germany. As World War II wound down, US troops captured what is believed to be about one-half of the images taken by *kriegsberichters*—the German equivalent of US signal corps photographers. These captured materials were housed at the US National Archives from 1947 until 1968, at which time they were shipped to the Federal Republic of Germany—but not until after copies had been made.

Beyond the invaluable help provided by the staffs of the National Archives and the Patton Museum, I am indebted to Tom Kailbourn, Scott Taylor, and Thomas Anderson. Their generous and skillful assistance adds immensely to the quality of this volume. I am especially blessed to have the faithful and tireless help of my wonderful wife, Denise, who has scanned thousands of photos and documents for this and numerous other books. Beyond that, she is an ongoing source of support and inspiration.

Contents

The *StuG III Ausf. G* was the ultimate model of the *Sturmgeschütz* assault gun, with production starting in December 1942. The *Ausf. G* was armed with the potent *StuK* 40 7.5 cm L/48 gun. This example was one of thirty the Germans transferred to the Finnish army in 1943. It was produced by Alkett in May or June 1943 and features 80 mm frontal armor on the hull and 50 mm basic armor with 30 mm armor bolted on in front of the driver's compartment. Small, fixed-front mud flaps and tubular, unreinforced fender supports are present. On the bow is the *hakaristi*, the Finnish national insignia, similar to the German *swastika*. On the frontal plate on the right side of the main gun is marked Ps. 531-5, the vehicle's Finnish identification number. *SA-Kuva*

CHAPTER 1

The *Sturmgeschütz Ausf. G* Is Introduced

The final upgrade to the *Sturmgeschütz* was the *Ausf. G*. With this model, the superstructure was completely revamped, although the chassis remained the same as that of the *Ausf. F/8* (described in *Sturmgeschütz,* Volume 1).

The superstructure was enlarged, the formerly short panniers now extending over the track guards for almost the entire length of the fighting compartment. The fighting compartment roof was raised slightly, and the commander now had a cupola as opposed to the earlier flat-panel hatches. The cupola included periscopes, as well as a mount for the *Scherenfernrohr* (scissors telescope).

As part of the so-called Adolf Hitler Armored Vehicle Program (Armored Vehicle Production Program III), drafted in September 1942, assault gun production was targeted at 300 vehicles per month, beginning in 1943. As part of this program, for the first time since Daimler-Benz built thirty-six *Sturmgeschütz Ausf.* As, a second firm joined with Alkett in producing the assault guns. That firm was Mühlenbau und Industrie A.-G., or MIAG. Further, to augment the chassis that MIAG produced themselves, Maschinenfabrik Augsburg Nürnberg (MAN) produced some chassis to supplement those being produced by MIAG in-house.

The *StuG* was the most-produced German armored vehicle, and the *Ausf. G* was far and away the most common version of the *Sturmgeschütz*, with output of this model exceeding the combined total of all prior models more than fivefold. Not surprisingly, given the number of *Ausf. G* built, and over a two-year production run, there were some variations of the type, as will be shown later in this volume.

CHAPTER 2
Alkett Production

American troops inspect a captured *StuG III Ausf. G* on a European battlefield. This vehicle was produced by Alkett between March and June 1944 and featured the cast mantlet with no opening for a coaxial machine gun used from October 1943 to September 1944. The track support rollers are the six-hole type introduced in January 1944, and the sprocket is the model without a hubcap or the central thread for mounting the hubcap, in use from March 1944 onward. The so-called waffle *Zimmerit*, an antimagnetic paste to repel magnetic mines with a waffle-like texture, is visible on the superstructure and the hull. Waffle *Zimmerit* was peculiar to Alkett vehicles produced from November 1943 to September 1944. *National Archives and Records Administration*

Production of the new type model *Sturmgeschütz* was begun at Alkett in December of 1942. The new *StuG Ausf. G* incorporated the chassis of the *Ausf. F/8*, itself being derived from the 8. Serie/ZW: the *Panzer III Ausf. J*.

The superstructure of the *Sturmgeschütz*, which had previously been enlarged with the introduction of the *Ausf. E*, was further enlarged, and the roof was raised slightly. At the center of the raised roof was an improved ventilator fan, needed to exhaust the fumes caused by firing the gun.

From the first month of production, a square machine gun shield was installed ahead of the loader's hatch, allowing an MG 34 to be factory installed on a *StuG*. The same type of shields were also later retrofitted to earlier models of *StuG*.

Atop the roof was mounted a rotating commander's cupola with seven periscopes. This cupola replaced the hatch system previously used by *Sturmgeschütz* commanders. A small opening with an armored cover was provided in the cupola hatch, through which a scissors periscope could be deployed.

While the cupola provided some operational benefits not found with the hatch system, at the same time it introduced a new vulnerability. It was found that the protruding cupola could be hit by antitank fire and penetrated, torn off, or driven into the fighting compartment. For this reason, in September 1943, Alkett began installing shell deflectors ahead of the cupolas.

A few months prior to that, in April 1943, Alkett began using hulls with 80 mm front armor, eliminating the need to bolt 30 mm supplemental armor plates to the 50-mm-thick base armor, as had been done on earlier models.

Spaced armor plates (*Schürzen*) began to be installed alongside the hull beginning in May 1943. These were added for protection against Russian antitank rifles but also were useful against hollow-charge ammunition as fired by bazookas and PIATs.

In October of 1943, Alkett introduced the cast mantlet, or *topfblende*, which translated literally means "pot mantlet." During the years since World War II, many have referred to the cast mantlet as *Saukopfblende*, or "pig's head" mantlet.

During May 1944, provisions for mounting an internally operated 360-degree traverse machine gun, or *rundumfeuer*, on the superstructure roof were added. This was to replace the previously used shielded MG 34. However, because the mounts themselves were not available, many of the mounting points were closed off.

The following month, a second machine gun mounting was added in the form of a coaxial machine gun. This MG 34 was installed on the left (driver's) side of the mantlet.

Alkett, a subsidiary of Rheinmetall-Borsig located in Berlin, produced the *Sturmgeschütz G* until April 25, 1945, a week before Berlin fell. It is worthwhile to point out that in addition to regular Alkett workers, almost 3,000 prisoners from Sachsenhausen concentration camp were forced to work in *Sturmgeschütz* production.

Two American GIs, including a tanker standing atop the superstructure, investigate a captured *StuG III Ausf. G* produced by Alkett in August 1944. The muzzle brake of the *StuK* 40 7.5 cm L/48 gun has been broken by a direct hit on the left side, and numerous hits have registered on the front of the hull. The muzzle brake is the type with an oval face and a circular rear ring: a feature on Alkett *StuG III Ausf. G*s produced from June to October 1944, hereafter referred to as the "oval/round muzzle." The vehicle had waffle *Zimmerit* and *Schürzen*: side skirts of 5 mm armor designed to detonate antitank shells before they struck the hull. More than twenty rings signifying kills are painted on the 7.5 cm gun barrel. A folded-down travel lock for the gun is on the front center of the glacis.
National Archives and Records Administration

This Alkett-manufactured *StuG III Ausf. G* hull with the superstructure removed has been pressed into use, apparently by Allied forces, pushing railroad cars at a port in the latter part of World War II. This type of sprocket with a hubcap was present on Alkett vehicles to March 1944, and the track-return rollers featuring six holes and no ribs were introduced in January 1944. A tow pintle, not a standard item, has been installed on the upper vertical rear plate of the hull. On the slanted rear plate above the tow pintle are two white identification stars and illegible markings. *National Archives and Records Administration*

The rear end of a *StuG III Ausf. G* of the *16th SS Panzergrenadier Division "Reichsführer-SS"* at a railroad yard is visible. A *Balkenkreuz* identification cross and SS runes are painted on the rear of the hull. To the far left, a tubular tail light is visible, a feature introduced into *StuG III Ausf. G* production in March 1943. At the bottom of the hull is a small, pivoting trailer tow coupling that was discontinued in March 1943. Thus, the production date of this vehicle can be dated to March 1943. A spare bogie wheel, a spare track section, and other equipment are stored on the rear deck. *Bundesarchiv*

This *StuG III Ausf. G* manufactured by Alkett in May or June 1943 is shown after receiving modifications for Finnish service. Factory-installed features include 30 mm bow armor bolted to the stock 50 mm armor and a rotating cupola. Prominent Finnish modifications include an armored cover for the driver's visor and concrete "armor" on the front of the superstructure. A shot deflector to the front of the cupola has been installed as a Finnish modification. Without the deflector, the vertical front of the cupola made for a vulnerable target for antitank rounds. The spare track sections on the bow are arranged in an interesting fashion, with coupled links on the bottom and individual links above. Some links have the late-type solid guides, while others have the perforated guides. *SA-Kuva*

A *StuG III Ausf. G* assigned to the German Army's *Sturmgeschütz Brigade 303* moves through a clearing in Finland around August 1944. This brigade was operating as the antitank reserve for the Finnish 3rd Infantry Division. This Alkett vehicle was built between June and August 1944, on the basis of the style of the oval/circular muzzle brake and the type of cast mantlet. Concrete armor has been added to the front of the superstructure; on the rest of the superstructure and the lower hull is waffle-pattern *Zimmerit*. The track support rollers have rubber tires and were installed on *StuG III Ausf. G*s at the factory until September 1944. *SA-Kuva*

Somewhere along the Gustav Line in Italy on May 23, 1944, two Tommies of the British Eighth Army observe two hits on the 80 mm armor bow of an Alkett *StuG III Ausf. G* produced in April or May 1943. The vehicle was knocked out by a Sherman tank. In other damage to the vehicle, the front of the mantlet has broken free from the sides, and the bolts on the left frontal plate of the superstructure have sheared off. Part of the fender has been blasted away, and one of the bogie wheels has broken away from its mount. Three smoke grenade launchers are on the side of the superstructure.
National Archives and Records Administration

Schürzen presented 5 mm of armor to detonate shaped-charge or high-explosive shells before they hit the vehicle, but these skirts did not always save a *StuG III* from serious damage or destruction. The right skirt on this *StuG III Ausf. G* has taken a hit from a large-caliber projectile and several smaller ones, crumpling the plates, riddling them with shrapnel, and creating radiating stress marks. No *Zimmerit* is present, suggesting this vehicle was produced in or after September 9, 1944, after which the factory application of *Zimmerit* to German tanks ceased. Atop the superstructure is the armored shield of a remote-control machine gun mount. *National Archives and Records Administration*

Waffle-pattern *Zimmerit* has been applied to this *StuG III Ausf. G* rolling through a town with signs in French on the buildings. The early-style rails and brackets for holding the armored skirts are present; this type of holder was factory installed from April 1943 to March 1944. A series of L-shaped fittings on the rails and also at the level of the fenders held the skirts in place; these fittings were inserted through holes in the skirts. The railing around the rear deck to hold baggage in place was installed at the Alkett factory from November 1943 to the end of production. The track support rollers are the type with steel rims, six holes, and spokes, installed on *StuG III Ausf. G*s on the Alkett assembly lines from November 1943 to March 1944. *National Archives and Records Administration*

The crew of an Alkett-produced *StuG III Ausf. G* poses for their photo next to a billboard with signs in Dutch. The vehicle is equipped with KGS 61/400/120 40 cm tracks with six chevrons on the treads; this type of track was factory installed on *StuG III Ausf. G*s from December 1943 to the end of production. This vehicle was produced no later than March 1944, as indicated by the early-type skirt rails and the six-holed, spoked track support rollers. Note the application of the waffle-pattern *Zimmerit* to the tops of the mudguards and the nearly square section of *Zimmerit* that has been knocked off on the side of the driver's compartment. *National Archives and Records Administration*

A *StuG III Ausf. G* produced by Alkett sometime between December 1943 and March 1944 exhibits waffle-pattern *Zimmerit* applied rather sloppily in grids that are slightly out of plumb. This photo provides a clear view of the early-type armored skirt rails and front brackets. Visible on the outboard side of the front of each of the rails is an upturned tab, one of several that held the armored skirt plates in place. In March 1944, improved skirt holders were introduced to the production lines with more rugged and dependable fasteners. *National Archives and Records Administration*

Details of the application patterns of the waffle-type *Zimmerit* around the driver's compartment and visor are apparent in this photo of a *StuG III Ausf. F* manufactured by Alkett between December 1943 and March 1944. To the front of the cupola is a shot deflector, introduced to the production lines in September 1943. *National Archives and Records Administration*

A Finnish *StuG III Ausf. G* lies at rest in a clearing. It exhibits waffle-pattern *Zimmerit*, concrete armor on the front of the superstructure, an armored visor cover, and bolted-on supplemental armor on the side of the hull. It was common practice for Finnish *StuG III*s to store three logs on each side of the superstructure to provide extra protection from fire from the sides. This vehicle was produced by Alkett between March and June 1944, as delimited by the shackle-type tow-cable holders with wing nuts on the forward ends of the fenders, introduced in March 1944, and the hinged machine gun shield, which was discontinued on the assembly lines in June 1944. *SA-Kuva*

British troops pause next to a *StuG III Ausf. G* manufactured by Alkett in July or August 1944. The travel lock on which the soldier is sitting was introduced in July 1944, while the early-type cast mantlet was last installed on *StuG III Ausf. G*s in August 1944. A multicolor camouflage is painted on the late-model armored skirts; the front skirt exhibits the so-called ambush pattern, with light-colored spots sprayed at intervals. *National Archives and Records Administration*

A *StuG III Ausf. G* manufactured by Alkett between October 1943 and March 1944 is in an ambush position, a camouflage blind fashioned from tall grass having been pulled back to the rear of the vehicle. It features the early-style armored skirts, a cast mantlet, and sprockets with hubcaps. A splotchy camouflage-paint scheme has been applied, and a dust cover is secured to the muzzle of the 7.5 cm gun. *National Archives and Records Administration*

Three *StuG III Ausf. G*s advance along a muddy road through a settlement during cold weather. The date of production of the closest one, an Alkett vehicle, can be narrowed down to October or November 1943, on the basis of the style of the cast mantlet and the lack of *Zimmerit*. It is equipped with six-chevron tracks, and a three-link section of track is attached to the right front of the superstructure. A large wooden crate is on the engine deck. The second vehicle and probably the third one too have concrete armor on the fronts of the superstructures. *National Archives and Records Administration*

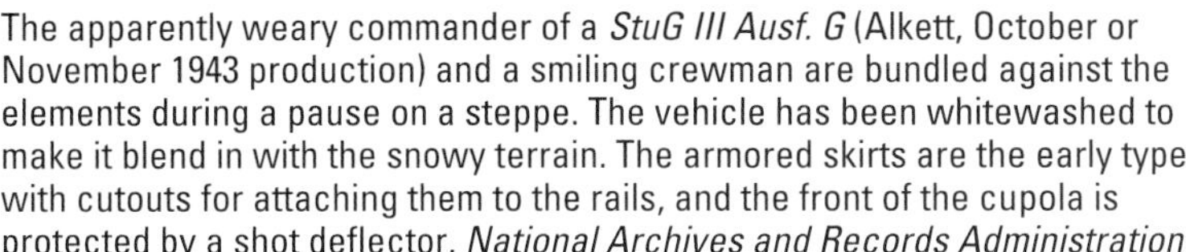

The apparently weary commander of a *StuG III Ausf. G* (Alkett, October or November 1943 production) and a smiling crewman are bundled against the elements during a pause on a steppe. The vehicle has been whitewashed to make it blend in with the snowy terrain. The armored skirts are the early type with cutouts for attaching them to the rails, and the front of the cupola is protected by a shot deflector. *National Archives and Records Administration*

The commander of a *StuG III Ausf. G*, apparently the same one depicted in the preceding photograph, scans the distance for signs of enemy activity. He is wearing a winter fur cap and a shearling coat. Atop the cupola to his front are the twin objectives of the scissors periscope. The cupola hatch is the type that was held open at an angle of 45 degrees: this model of hatch was found from the beginning of *Ausf. G* production to June 1944. *National Archives and Records Administration*

As the year 1944 advanced, the Allies gained air superiority over the battlefields of Normandy, and fighter-bombers became a constant threat to armored columns on the roads of France. This *StuG III Ausf. G* with waffle *Zimmerit* and a passenger car bedecked with foliage camouflage have taken cover under the trees along a country road. The *StuG* was produced between February 1944, when the drive sprocket without the hubcap was introduced to the assembly line, and August 1944, when the model of cast mantlet seen here was discontinued. *National Archives and Records Administration*

Soldiers are looking intently at the running gear of a well-camouflaged *StuG III Ausf. G* that is beginning to move ahead slowly, possibly after a hasty roadside repair. Alkett produced this vehicle in March 1944: it features the six-hole, spoked track support rollers that were discontinued from *StuG III* production in March 1944, and the triangular brackets for the armored skirts that were introduced to the assembly lines in March 1944. One of these brackets is visible on the edge of the fender between the sprocket and the first track support roller. *National Archives and Records Administration*

The armored skirts on this *StuG III Ausf. G* on the western front feature rounded bottoms for a scalloped effect. The foliage camouflage has been extended to include the 7.5 cm gun barrel. This machine was manufactured at Alkett between February and June 1944. The sprocket with no hubcap was introduced to production in February 1944, while the hinged machine gun shield was discontinued in June 1944. Concrete armor has been installed above the driver's compartment, and a very close examination of the photo reveals that waffle-pattern *Zimmerit* is present. *National Archives and Records Administration*

A *StuG III Ausf. G* with a partial camouflage treatment of whitewash over a base color, likely *Dunkelgelb*, advances along a snowy road. Two sections of the early-type armored skirts are suspended from the left side of the vehicle. Sometimes the skirt plates shook loose from the vehicles, or they were discarded when damaged or shot up. The month of production of this *StuG* can be established as October 1943: this style of cast mantlet came into production that month, and the vehicle lacks *Zimmerit*, which Alkett began applying to its *StuG III Ausf. G*s in November 1943. *National Archives and Records Administration*

A *Sturmgeschütz* column hugs the right side of a road through a settlement evidently on the Eastern Front, avoiding a muddy, heavily rutted lane on the left. The number "127" is painted on the side of the superstructure and on the armor skirt of the nearest vehicle, a *StuG III Ausf. G* produced by Alkett between March and June 1944, on the basis of the late-type skirt brackets dating to March 1944 and later, and the presence of a hinged machine gun shield, discontinued from production at Alkett in June 1944. On the rear deck are a rail for retaining baggage, a large stowage box, and a spare bogie wheel. *National Archives and Records Administration*

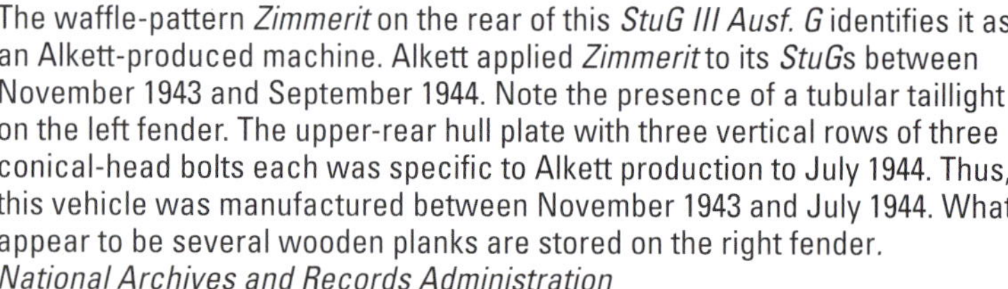

The waffle-pattern *Zimmerit* on the rear of this *StuG III Ausf. G* identifies it as an Alkett-produced machine. Alkett applied *Zimmerit* to its *StuG*s between November 1943 and September 1944. Note the presence of a tubular taillight on the left fender. The upper-rear hull plate with three vertical rows of three conical-head bolts each was specific to Alkett production to July 1944. Thus, this vehicle was manufactured between November 1943 and July 1944. What appear to be several wooden planks are stored on the right fender. *National Archives and Records Administration*

Waffen-SS officers confer next to a *StuG III Ausf. G* built by Alkett between May and October 1943. Alkett used the pressed-steel fender supports as seen here from May 1943 onward, and discontinued the screwed mantlet in October 1943. Details are visible of the Notek blackout headlight, the glacis access hatch hinges, the fender with its nonslip texture, the fixed mud flap, and the bolted frontal armor of the driver's compartment. *SA-Kuva*

Sturmgeschütz Ausf. G	
Make	Alkett
Chassis (Fgst) number	91651–94250, 105001 to approx. 108940
Quantity	about 5,840
Dimensions	
Length	22′ 2½″
Width	9′ 7″
Height	7′ 3/4″
Weight	23.9 tons

Performance	
Maximum speed	25 mph
Cruising speed	12.5 mph
Cross-country	6 mph
Range, on road	99 miles
Range, cross-country	62 miles
Trench crossing	7.5′
Crew	4
Communications	Fu 16 or Fu 15

Armament	
Weapon, main	7.5 cm *StuK* L/48
Secondary	2 x 7.92 mm MG 34
Elevation	-10 to +20 degrees
Traverse	12 degrees right; 12 degrees left
Ammo stowage, main	54 rounds
7.92 mm	600 rounds
Automotive	
Engine make	Maybach
Engine model	HL 120 TRM
Engine configuration	V-12, liquid cooled
Engine displacement	11.9 liters
Engine horsepower	265 @ 2,600 rpm
Fuel capacity	82 gallons
Transmission	SSG 77
Speeds	6 + reverse
Steering	differential
Track	Kgs 61/400/120
Links per side	93

StuG III Ausf. G license number WH-0170343 is observed from the rear. This vehicle, chassis number 92112, was delivered to the *Wehrmacht* by Alkett in March 1943. On the ventilator covers on the rear deck are steel-rimmed bogie wheels. Alkett mounted this type of bogie wheels experimentally on a *StuG III Ausf. G* in late 1944. Between the spare bogie wheels is a toolbox. Spare track sections, six links on the left and four on the right, are stowed to the sides of the round ventilator on the rear of the superstructure. The oblong object to the left of center on the rear of the hull is the cover for the engine-starter crank fitting. *Patton Museum*

A column of *StuG III*s serve as battle taxis for German troops during a winter campaign. On the tank to the front, the cast mantlet, the late-type armor skirts, and the absence of *Zimmerit* indicate that the vehicle was built by Alkett in October or November 1944. Note the askew position of the front plate of the armor skirt and the absence of a rear plate. *Patton Museum*

With assistance from a truck-mounted boom crane and guidance from two soldiers, a *StuK* 40 7.5 cm L/48 gun is being hoisted from a *StuG III Ausf. G*. The gun, mantlet, and carriage could be removed from the vehicle as a unit. Alkett produced this particular vehicle between April and June 1943, on the basis of the 80 mm bow armor (30 mm supplemental armor welded to 50 mm armor), which Alkett instituted on *Ausf. G* production in April 1943, and the presence of unreinforced tubular fender supports, which Alkett installed on these vehicles until June 1943. *Patton Museum*

The temporary insignia of the *11th Panzer Division* is on the left side of the bow of this *StuG III Ausf. G* advancing across a steppe. This insignia consisted of three vertical lines with a horizontal line across the bottom. The convergence of two specific features, the presence of early-model armor skirts and the bolted supplemental armor on the bow and the front of the superstructure, make it possible to identify the month Alkett produced this vehicle: April 1943. A dust cover is present over the box-type, screwed mantlet assembly. *Patton Museum*

American soldiers inspect a captured *StuG III Ausf. G* that had been assigned to the *103rd Panzer Battalion, 3rd Panzergrenadier Division*. Alkett produced this vehicle, chassis number 92375, in May 1943, and that date of manufacture is in accord with the integral 80 mm welded bow armor, which the factory instituted in April 1943, and the presence of smoke grenade launchers, which Alkett discontinued in May 1943. Only the top tube is present on the smoke grenade launcher mount seen here. Unusual features include the positioning of the tow hook on the right front of the superstructure and the presence of a spare bogie wheel on the side of the superstructure. *National Archives and Records Administration*

Two Canadian soldiers take stock of a *StuG III Ausf. G* with a destroyed right suspension. The vehicle's chassis number, 97721, is painted in small numbers on the right front plate of the superstructure. Alkett produced this machine in April or May 1943, as indicated by the presence of integral 80 mm bow armor and smoke grenade launchers. The rear of the armored skirt rail has been twisted, and its rear bracket has been torn from the superstructure. The right track is the late type with perforated guide horns, while the spare track links on the holder on the bow mostly have solid guide horns, but two have perforated horns. *National Archives and Records Administration*

A first-series *StuG III Ausf. G* produced by Alkett starting in December 1942 advances across a steppe on the Eastern Front. It was only in the first-series *Ausf. G*s that the ventilator was on the roof of the superstructure, and this feature is visible between the two hatches. Faintly visible on the left mudguard is the tactical symbol for a *Sturmgeschütz* company that was introduced in 1943: a rhomboid with an upward-pointing arrow superimposed on the upper left. This model of *Ausf. G* lacked a machine gun shield for the loader, but this vehicle has a pintle mount for an MG 34 to the front of the loader's hatch. *National Archives and Records Administration*

A large wooden crate is on the rear deck of a *StuG III Ausf. G* on the Eastern Front. Large, hinged mud flaps are present; these were discontinued on the Alkett production line in March 1943. The tubular taillight seen on the left fender was introduced in March 1943. Hence, this vehicle seems to have been manufactured in March 1943. Early-type armored skirts are installed. The numerals in the number "211" on the rear of the hull indicate, left to right, 2nd Company, 1st Platoon, 1st vehicle.
National Archives and Records Administration

A *StuG III Ausf. G* of April or May 1943 production is poised next to a trench on a battlefield on the Eastern Front. This vehicle has the early-style skirts—specifically, the variety with the upper and lower panels in the second and third positions—but the two lower skirt panels are missing. Because of the rather tentative manner in which the early-style skirt brackets held the armored panels in place, the panels were easily jarred off or knocked off when the vehicle brushed against obstacles. Note the three irregularly shaped holes in the rear panel of the skirt. *National Archives and Records Administration*

Two members of a mortar platoon trudge alongside a *StuG III Ausf. G*. This is an Alkett first-series *Ausf. G*, as indicated by the ventilator on the superstructure roof and the steeply sloped "shoulder" on the side of the superstructure to the rear of the driver's compartment. This vehicle is equipped with *Winterketten*: special tracks with extended outboard sides to provide additional traction and flotation on snow and soft ground. *National Archives and Records Administration*

A *StuG III* with waffle *Zimmerit* and a *PzKpfw III* are parked together on a steppe. The *StuG* exhibits characteristics that narrow the parameters of its production date to between November 1943 and March 1944: the waffle-pattern *Zimmerit* made its appearance on the *StuG III* in November 1943, and the drive sprockets with hubcaps were discontinued from production at Alkett in March 1944.
National Archives and Records Administration

StuG III Ausf. G crews inspect and make adjustments to their vehicles in a shop setting in France in early 1944. At least the first three vehicles have waffle-pattern *Zimmerit.* All of the vehicles have cast mantlets and hinged machine gun shields. The nearest and the third vehicles have the early-style skirt brackets, while the second *StuG* has the late type. *Patton Museum*

Two *StuG III Ausf. G*s make their way along a hillside road, probably during the autumn of 1944. The lead vehicle was produced in June 1944, as indicated by two concurrent features: the hinged machine gun shield (seen here in the lowered position), which was discontinued on the Alkett production line in June 1944, and the oval/circular muzzle brake, which was introduced to *StuG III Ausf. G*s at Alkett in June 1944. The late-type armored skirts and brackets are installed. *Patton Museum*

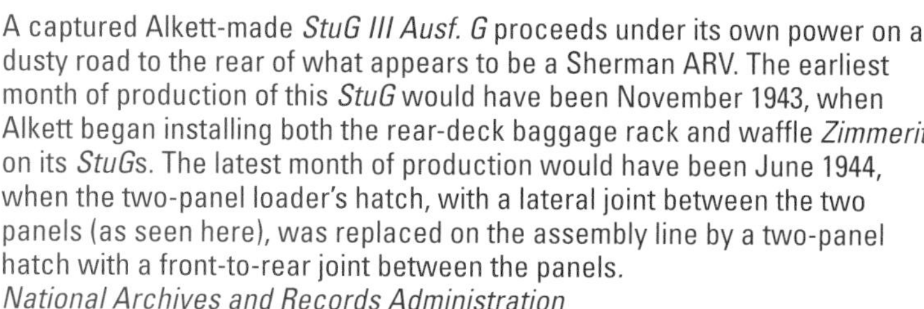

A captured Alkett-made *StuG III Ausf. G* proceeds under its own power on a dusty road to the rear of what appears to be a Sherman ARV. The earliest month of production of this *StuG* would have been November 1943, when Alkett began installing both the rear-deck baggage rack and waffle *Zimmerit* on its *StuG*s. The latest month of production would have been June 1944, when the two-panel loader's hatch, with a lateral joint between the two panels (as seen here), was replaced on the assembly line by a two-panel hatch with a front-to-rear joint between the panels.
National Archives and Records Administration

Two Canadian soldiers are surveying a *StuG III Ausf. G* knocked out or abandoned in Elbeuf, France, in late August 1944. The vehicle has waffle-pattern *Zimmerit*, a cast mantlet, and well-worn tracks with the chevron treads ground off. Alkett produced this *StuG* between January and March 1944: the six-hole, steel-rimmed track support rollers seen here were introduced to the production lines in January 1944, and the model of drive sprocket with the hubcap was discontinued in March of that year. Jammed against the rear of the *StuG* is an *SdKfz 251/9* armed with a 7.5 cm KwK 37 short-barreled gun. *National Archives and Records Administration*

German infantrymen clad in white reversible camouflage suits pose on and next to a whitewash-camouflaged *StuG III Ausf. G*. This Alkett vehicle was likely produced in April 1943: it features the integral 80 mm armor on the bow introduced to Alkett's *StuG III Ausf. G* assembly lines in April 1943, but lacks the armor skirts introduced at Alkett that same month. Note the ice cleats fastened to the tracks at intervals. *National Archives and Records Administration*

A *StuG III Ausf. G* wearing a winter whitewash camouflage emerges from a shed. The tracks are a model introduced in July 1944 and installed on some *StuG III Ausf. G*s until the end of the war. It featured only four diagonal cleats on the treads, with only the center two actually forming a chevron. For added traction, some detachable ice cleats have been mounted on the track, and one of them is clearly visible on the front of the left track assembly. *National Archives and Records Administration*

*StuG III Ausf. G*s roll past the wreckage of a vehicle during the Kursk Campaign in the summer of 1943. On the glacis of the closest *StuG* is the temporary insignia of *2nd SS Panzergrenadier Division "Das Reich"* used during this campaign. It was white and consisted of two vertical bars and a horizontal bar at the bottom. Barely visible on the left side of this insignia is the tactical symbol for the 3rd company of a *Sturmgeschütz* unit. This vehicle was produced by Alkett between December 1942 and February 1943. *National Archives and Records Administration*

A *StuG III Ausf. G* occupies a position near a river in the lowlands of France. Sprayed over the *Dunkelgelb* base color are splotches of a darker color, likely green or brown. The loader is manning an MG 42 supported by a bipod. Waffle-pattern *Zimmerit* is present on the hull, the superstructure, and the driver's visor. Note the variation in tone of the paint on the first two armor skirt panels versus the third, lighter-colored, panel. *National Archives and Records Administration*

The same *StuG III Ausf. G* as the one in the preceding photo is seen from a different angle alongside a river in France, probably in the late summer or early fall of 1944. This *StuG* bears features consistent with a production timeframe of July or August 1944. The style of cast mantlet seen here was discontinued at the Alkett factory in August 1944, and the travel lock at the front of the glacis was introduced to *StuG III Ausf. G* production at Alkett in July 1944. *National Archives and Records Administration*

A mouth full of fangs and an eye have been painted on the cast turret of this Alkett *StuG III Ausf. G*. Several indicators point to a production timeframe of June 1944: no travel lock is present as these were introduced on Alkett *StuG III Ausf. G*s in July 1944, while the style of muzzle brake seen close-up in this photo was introduced in June 1944. *National Archives and Records Administration*

The commander of this *StuG III Ausf. G* is wearing a paratrooper (*Fallschirmjäger*) helmet: an indication that this vehicle may have served with a *Luftwaffe Fallschirmjäger Division*, which fielded a variety of armored vehicles. This vehicle was produced by Alkett sometime between November 1943 and June 1944, judging by the presence of waffle-pattern *Zimmerit*, an early-type cast mantlet, and a folding machine gun shield. *National Archives and Records Administration*

A *StuG III Ausf. G* pauses during operations with a *PzKpfw III* to the left and an *SdKfz 263 8-rad Panzerfunkwagen* to the right. The month Alkett produced this *StuG* can be determined as April 1943. This is based on the presence of several features, including the early-type armored skirts, which Alkett began installing in April 1943, and the sprockets with hubcaps, which were discontinued that month. The muzzle brake on the 7.5 cm gun is the so-called "acorn" type, with a narrow front ring. *National Archives and Records Administration*

Replenishment of the 7.5 cm ammunition is underway on a steppe. The crewmen at the center and to the left are wearing reversible camouflage parkas and overalls. The front panel of the armored skirt has a camouflage pattern that appears to have been smeared on with a rag. Wire has been wound around the holders for the early-style skirts to keep them from jouncing off. Four steel helmets are strapped to the spare tracks on the rear of the superstructure. As a modification to hold up a section of spare track, three L-shaped brackets had been welded to the rear of the engine deck. Spare track pins are stuck into the lug holes in the spare bogie wheel to the left. *National Archives and Records Administration*

The waffle-pattern *Zimmerit* on this Alkett *StuG III Ausf. G* marks it as having been produced as early as November 1943, while the early-type armor skirt rails and the steel-rimmed, spoked, six-hole track support rollers are consistent for an Alkett vehicle manufactured up to March 1944. *Patton Museum*

These *StuG III Ausf. G* crewmen evidently are making preparations to camouflage their closely parked vehicles in a farmyard by stacking straw against them and applying tarpaulins. The presence of the early-type cast mantlet coupled with the lack of *Zimmerit* was peculiar to Alkett *StuG III Ausf. G*s manufactured in October 1943. Both vehicles' cupolas have the shot deflectors, which Alkett began introducing to its *StuG III Ausf. G*s in September 1943. *Patton Museum*

CHAPTER 3

Mühlenbau und Industrie A.-G. (MIAG) Production

In addition to Alkett, MIAG was the other producer of *StuG III Ausf. G*s. A British or Commonwealth tanker prepares to enter the cupola of a *StuG III Ausf. G* captured in or near Battipaglia, Italy, in September 1943. The chassis number of the vehicle is still visible in small numerals on the right frontal plate of the superstructure: 95219. MIAG completed this vehicle in April or May 1943. This vehicle was shipped to Aberdeen Proving Ground, Maryland, USA, and later was sent to Canada, where it finished its days as a target vehicle. *National Archives and Records Administration*

Due to Hitler's orders, by 1943, demand for *Sturmgeschütz* was increasing, while requirements for tanks were decreasing. Thus, with production of the *Panzer III* by MIAG winding down, that plant's capacity was transferred into producing the *Sturmgeschütz G*, supplementing those produced by Alkett.

Beginning in February 1943, ninety-eight *Panzer III* hulls on hand at MIAG were prepared for assembly as *Sturmgeschütz* instead and were integrated into *StuG* production along with conventional *StuG* chassis.

As part of the conversion, 30 mm armor plates were bolted to the 50 mm integral front hull plate of the tank hulls in order to bring them up to the 80 mm armor standard for assault gun chassis.

In order to accelerate production even further, the MIAG-assembled chassis were supplemented with 142 chassis produced by Maschinenfabrik Augsburg Nürnberg (MAN). In fact, even during the first month of *Sturmgeschütz* production at MIAG, MAN chassis were used in addition to the firm's own *StuG* chassis. The former *Panzer III* hulls began to be used in April.

Production at MIAG was largely uninterrupted during 1943, allowing production to climb from ten in February to 138 in October, with the 1943 year total being 1,168.

In February 1944, the plant was subjected to the first of five aerial attacks it would suffer through May of that year. These raids severely hampered production, with the first raid costing 25% of the month's output.

New vehicle production was also affected by the directive that over 100 complete *Panzer III* be converted to *Sturmgeschütz*; this work was done from April through August.

While most of the changes made by Alkett during production of the *Sturmgeschütz Ausf. G* were also made by MIAG, there were some exceptions. While Alkett was able to use hulls with integral 80 mm frontal armor from April 1943 onward, MIAG had to continue bolting on supplemental armor until November 1943, only to resume again in May/June 1944, during the conversion of *Panzer III* to *Sturmgeschütz*.

The distinctive cast-steel mantlet introduced in October 1943 was uniquely an Alkett feature; MIAG *StuG*s exclusively used mantlets of bolted construction.

MIAG delivered, and the German army accepted, a number of *Sturmgeschütz,* with the commander's cupola erroneously welded in place backwards during early 1943. Also, the round deflector, added ahead of the cupola in September 1943 by Alkett, was not introduced into MIAG production until December of that year.

Following a bomb raid on the MIAG plant in March 1945, causing severe damage, *Sturmgeschütz* production by the firm came to an end.

This MIAG *StuG Ausf. G* is serving as a battle taxi for Hungarian troops operating alongside German forces on the Eastern Front. The presence of all-steel, spoked track support rollers without holes, introduced to the MIAG production lines in November 1943, and drive sprockets with the central thread for holding a hubcap plugged, which were discontinued in November 1944, establish the timeframe of this vehicle's completion as November 1943 to January 1944. On the side of the superstructure, Soviet T-34 tank tracks have been installed for added protection. *National Archives and Records Administration*

American soldiers pore over a captured *StuG III Ausf. G*; another *StuG III Ausf. G* is parked alongside it. A rare view is available of the interior side of the left engine-access hatch, with its two elongated ventilation openings. The vehicle in the foreground has the early-style skirt brackets, which MIAG began using in April 1943. *Zimmerit* has not been applied, so this vehicle was completed prior to September 1943. The rotating cupola lacked a shot deflector. *National Archives and Records Administration*

Supply troops are replenishing the ammunition of a *StuG III Ausf. G* with no *Zimmerit* applied. Note the ammunition boxes and packing tubes to the left and the large storage box on the engine deck. The tactical number "351" is visible on the skirt. This vehicle was at the earliest produced in April 1943, as indicated by presence of early-type armored skirts, and at the latest in September 1943, when MIAG began applying *Zimmerit* to these vehicles at the factory. *National Archives and Records Administration*

From September to December 1943, MIAG applied to its *StuG III Ausf. G*s a distinctive pattern of *Zimmerit* featuring tightly spaced crosshatches. This overhead photo of a *StuG III Ausf. G* whitewashed for winter operations depicts the MIAG *Zimmerit* on the face and sides of the superstructure. The photo also shows details of the top of the superstructure, including the gunner's periscopic sight and its sliding cover; the cupola, surrounded by track links for added protection; and the folded-down machine gun shield. *National Archives and Records Administration*

The left access hatches on the glacis of a MIAG *StuG III Ausf. G* are open, offering a rare view of their interior, including the hinges and the two locking handles on the inboard hatch door. This image also offers a close-up view of the MIAG style of *Zimmerit* application. *National Archives and Records Administration*

Crewmen are replenishing the 7.5 cm ammunition of a MIAG-built *StuG III Ausf. G* at a site in Italy by passing rounds from a storage magazine inside the building. The latching mechanism on the rear panel of the loader's hatch is in view, and details of the front panel are visible in the foreground. On the rear of the engine deck is a set of spare bogie wheels with spare track pins stuck into them. On the rear of the right fender is the jack block. *National Archives and Records Administration*

The same *StuG III Ausf. G* shown in the preceding photo is seen from another angle as crewmen continue to pass 7.5 cm ammunition. This vehicle is from MIAG's November 1943 to May 1944 production, on the basis of the presence of steel six-spoke track support rollers, introduced to MIAG production in November 1943, and the style of loader's hatch with a lateral division between the two panels, which was discontinued in May 1944 in favor of a hatch with a fore-and-aft divide. Note the dark-colored engine starter crank on the rear of the hull. *National Archives and Records Administration*

StuG III Ausf. Gs are loaded on flatcars for long-distance transport while another *StuG III Ausf. G* is parked on the ground. The closest vehicle exhibits MIAG-style *Zimmerit*, early-style armor skirt brackets, and six-spoked steel track support rollers. These features suggest the vehicle was produced between November 1943, when MIAG began using that style of track support rollers, to March 1944, when the late-type skirt brackets were introduced. The dust covers on these vehicles spanned the front of the superstructure and included an opening for the driver's visor.
National Archives and Records Administration

Two *StuG III Ausf. G*s are passing by steel road obstacles shoved to the side of a street on the edge of a town. The closest vehicle has the crosshatched *Zimmerit* of a MIAG-built machine. The six-chevron tracks were installed on *StuG III Ausf. G*s at the MIAG factory starting in December 1943, while MIAG continued to install the early-style armored skirt holders until March 1944. Thus, the closest vehicle was produced between December 1943 and March 1944. On the rear plate of the hull are two clamps for holding a starter handle. *National Archives and Records Administration*

A *StuG III Ausf. G* is entering a breach in a roadside wall while another one awaits its turn to advance. The nearer vehicle exhibits MIAG-style *Zimmerit* and tubular fender supports. The earliest month of production of this vehicle can be established as November 1943, when the solid-steel, spoked track support wheels without six holes were introduced. The latest month of production would have been March 1944, when the late-type armor skirts and their brackets were introduced. Note the diagonally positioned fire extinguisher and the tubular taillight on the rear of the left fender. *National Archives and Records Administration*

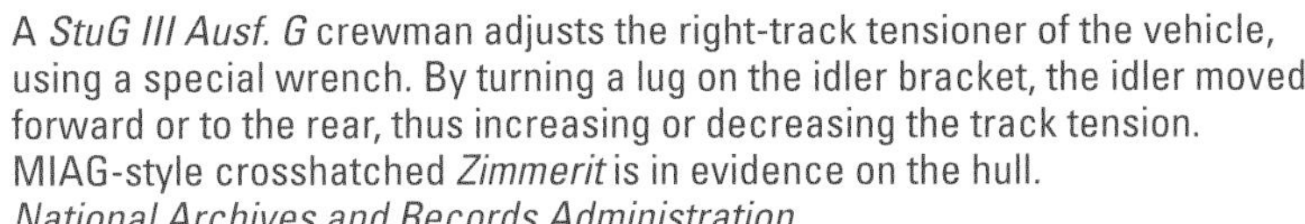

A *StuG III Ausf. G* crewman adjusts the right-track tensioner of the vehicle, using a special wrench. By turning a lug on the idler bracket, the idler moved forward or to the rear, thus increasing or decreasing the track tension. MIAG-style crosshatched *Zimmerit* is in evidence on the hull. *National Archives and Records Administration*

Constant lubrication of the running gear of the *StuG III Ausf. G* was necessary to prevent breakdowns. Here, a crewman uses a grease gun to lubricate one of the track support rollers. The rollers are of the solid-steel, six-spoked model with no holes, which MIAG used on its *StuG III Ausf. G*s from November 1943 until the end of production. The bogie wheels remained constant in design throughout *StuG III* production from June 1940 to the end of production. They were fitted with rubber tires from a number of manufacturers, including Continental, DEKA, Dunlop, Fulda, Metzeler, Semperit, and Vorwerk. MIAG-type *Zimmerit* is visible on the hull. *National Archives and Records Administration*

Two *Sturmgeschütz* crewmen stand next to their vehicle, which exhibits MIAG-style *Zimmerit*. They are wearing field-gray M43 *Einheitsfeldmütze* caps and *Panzer* uniforms consisting of double-breasted field-gray jackets and matching trousers. The officer to the left is wearing the Iron Cross First Class, the ribbon for the Iron Cross Second Class, the General Assault Badge, and a campaign ribbon. *National Archives and Records Administration*

A *StuG III Ausf. G* with MIAG-type *Zimmerit* is viewed from the front right. The vehicle is heavily weathered: note the light-colored staining down the frontal panel of the superstructure. Early-style armor skirts are mounted; note the wire for locking the plates in place on their brackets. Mounted on the early-type folding shield is an MG 34. This type of sprocket with the threaded socket for holding a hubcap removed and plugged was specific to MIAG production from November 1943 to January 1944. A heavy-duty, C-type tow hook is attached to the right tow fitting on the hull.
National Archives and Records Administration

Hungarian soldiers march alongside a German-operated *StuG III Ausf. G* on the Eastern Front. The finely crosshatched *Zimmerit* characteristic of MIAG-produced *StuG III Ausf. Gs* is evident. Here again, this vehicle has the type of sprockets with plugged threads that were specific to MIAG production from November 1943 to January 1944. Early-style skirts and brackets are present. The commander is wearing a caped coat, likely a motorcycle rider's all-weather overcoat.
National Archives and Records Administration

Sturmgeschütz crewmen are seated on the front of a *StuG III Ausf. G*. The armored skirts are the late type with triangular brackets, introduced to MIAG *StuG III Ausf. Gs* in March 1944. The hinged machine gun shield was discontinued at MIAG in May 1944. Hence, this vehicle dates to March, April, or May 1944. Note the logs stowed on the right side of the superstructure. A nonstandard bracket of unknown purpose is protruding from the glacis adjacent to the Notek blackout headlight.
National Archives and Records Administration

Sturmgeschütz Ausf. G	
Make	MIAG
Chassis (Fgst) number	MIAG-built chassis 95001–97586, MAN chassis 76126–76210; 77351–77408
Quantity	2,728
Dimensions	
Length	22′ 2½″
Width	9′ 7″
Height	7′ 3/4″
Weight	23.9 tons
Performance	
Maximum speed	25 mph
Cruising speed	12.5 mph
Cross-country	6 mph
Range, on road	99 miles
Range, cross-country	62 miles
Trench crossing	7.5′
Crew	4
Communications	Fu 16 or Fu.15
Armament	
Weapon, main	7.5 cm *StuK* L/48
Secondary	2 x 7.92 mm MG 34
Elevation	-10 to +20 degrees
Traverse	12 degrees right; 12 degrees left
Ammo stowage, main	54 rounds
7.92 mm	600 rounds
Automotive	
Engine make	Maybach
Engine model	HL 120 TRM
Engine configuration	V-12, liquid cooled
Engine displacement	11.9 liters
Engine horsepower	265 @ 2,600 rpm
Fuel capacity	82 gallons
Transmission	SSG 77
Speeds	6 + reverse
Steering	differential
Track	Kgs 61/400/120
Links per side	93

A close examination of the same *StuG III Ausf. G* shown in the preceding photo, at the same time and place, reveals a finely applied, squiggly camouflage pattern on the armored skirt, as well as the number "101" in a dark-colored paint with white borders. On the glacis is a section of spare track with a track pin partially pulled out. *Patton Museum*

A *StuG III Ausf. G* has come alongside a truck to receive fuel. In the rear of the truck a soldier is seated, ready to operate a hand crank to pump fuel from a drum next to him. A crewman on the engine deck of the *StuG* is handling the fuel hose. MIAG produced this vehicle in the summer of 1943. Barely visible on the rear of the hull are a very faded number "10°" in white outline and a *Balkenkreuz*, black with white outlining. To the left of the *Balkenkreuz* is painted a light-colored square with two small Maltese crosses on it. This apparently was a variant of the insignia of the 244th *Sturmgeschütz* Battalion. A carrying case and several pieces of lumber are stuffed between the skirt and the superstructure.
National Archives and Records Administration

On the southern front in Russia, Hungarian soldiers are hitching a ride on a German-operated *StuG III Ausf. G* with the typical MIAG-style *Zimmerit*. The month of production of this *StuG* may be narrowed down to between November 1943 and January 1944. It features sprockets with the threaded socket for the hubcap plugged, early-style armored skirts, a folding machine gun shield, and tubular fender supports. Tall grass has been hung on the skirts, hull, and superstructure for camouflage purposes. *Patton Museum*

In a photo related to the preceding one, Hungarian infantrymen board a *StuG III Ausf. G* while another *StuG III* laden with troops advances in the background. This vehicle is probably from September 1943 production, featuring MIAG *Zimmerit*, early-style skirts, and a starter crank on the rear of the hull. That location for the starter crank dates to the summer of 1943. *Patton Museum*

An American GI pauses to investigate a knocked-out *StuG III Ausf. G*. The lack of *Zimmerit* and the presence of early-style armor skirts and brackets point to a date of completion for this vehicle of April to September 1943. Dual bogie wheel assemblies were stored two high on the rear ventilator covers. Note the angled positioning of the fire extinguisher and the presence of a Notek box-type taillight, also referred to as a distance indicator, on the rear of the left fender. This style of taillight was factory installed on MIAG *StuG III Ausf. G*s from February 1943 to December 1943.
National Archives and Records Administration

In a photograph dated September 20, 1943, British personnel ride on a *StuG III Ausf. G* that the Germans abandoned in the Salerno area of Italy. A jack is resting on the front of the vehicle. This *StuG* was manufactured in April or May 1943, as determined by the early-style skirts, which dated to April 1943, and the presence of grenade launchers, which were discontinued in May 1943. Bolted onto the front of the hull are 30 mm supplemental armor plates; these were applied over the stock 50 mm frontal armor. *National Archives and Records Administration*

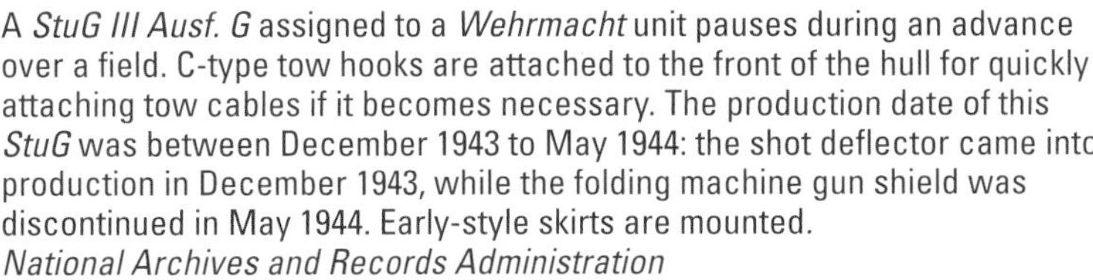

A *StuG III Ausf. G* assigned to a *Wehrmacht* unit pauses during an advance over a field. C-type tow hooks are attached to the front of the hull for quickly attaching tow cables if it becomes necessary. The production date of this *StuG* was between December 1943 to May 1944: the shot deflector came into production in December 1943, while the folding machine gun shield was discontinued in May 1944. Early-style skirts are mounted. *National Archives and Records Administration*

A good view is available of the MIAG factory-applied, crosshatched *Zimmerit* on a *StuG III Ausf. G*. The raised portions of the *Zimmerit* were quite rough in texture, and the grooves that composed the crosshatching were applied in more or less straight lines. The cupola lacks a shot deflector, which means the vehicle was produced before December 1943, and the presence of factory *Zimmerit* means the vehicle was produced in or after September 1943. The hinged panel with a welded grab handle that is mounted on the cupola hatch dates to October 1943 and later. *National Archives and Records Administration*

A *Sturmgeschütz* column advances along a dirt road. The lead vehicle has an indistinguishable, shield-type insignia on the left side of the glacis. The month of production of this *StuG III Ausf. G* was September 1943, on the basis of two considerations: there is no shot deflector (these fixtures were installed at the MIAG factory from September 1943 onward), and MIAG-style *Zimmerit* is present, a feature that was instituted in September 1943. *National Archives and Records Administration*

The crew of this *StuG III Ausf. G* was aiming for maximum concealment of their vehicle through the use of local camouflage in the form of tree branches. On the basis of the visible evidence, this machine was produced between February 1943, when MIAG commenced the installation of welded 30 mm supplemental bow armor, and June 1943, when the acorn-type muzzle brake was discontinued. Note the sharply delineated camouflage paint on the 7.5 cm gun barrel.
National Archives and Records Administration

Two *StuG III Ausf. G*s have paused during operations. A crewman on the rear vehicle is handling a tow cable, so evidently one of the vehicles was or is in need of assistance. The armored skirt panels on the *StuG* to the front are of interest. The first three panels have *Zimmerit* applied: a rare occurrence to see in photographs. The front panel has a raked pattern, with wide vertical rows of horizontally ridged *Zimmerit*. The second and third panels have the typical MIAG tightly spaced crosshatch pattern. The rear panel has no *Zimmerit*. *National Archives and Records Administration*

In some cases, *Zimmerit* was applied to armored vehicles in the field rather than at the factory. Such was the case with this MIAG *StuG III Ausf. G*, which has a raked *Zimmerit* unlike the waffle and crosshatched patterns applied at the factory by Alkett and MIAG, respectively. This vehicle was produced in April or May 1943, on the basis of the presence of early-type armor skirts and smoke grenade launchers. Note the 7.5 cm rounds laid on the mantlet and the superstructure roof.
National Archives and Records Administration

Preparations to recover this mired *StuG III Ausf. G* have just begun, as crewmen on the far side of the bow prepare a tow cable. Evidence of MIAG-style *Zimmerit* is visible on the bow. This vehicle was from November 1943 to January 1944 production. *National Archives and Records Administration*

Foliage has been piled in front of this *StuG III Ausf. G* for concealment in its exposed position in an open field. A horseshoe has been propped up against the Notek blackout headlight for extra luck. The *Zimmerit* on the bow is unusual in that it is the MIAG closely spaced crosshatch pattern, but it has been applied diagonally rather than in vertical columns and horizontal rows.
National Archives and Records Administration

The 7.5 cm gun of this *StuG III Ausf. G* has just been fired, and the barrel is in recoil. A dark-colored dust cover is fitted over the mantlet, in contrast to the overall *Dunkelgelb* paint scheme of the vehicle. Early-style armored skirts are mounted. The cupola hatch is open at a 45-degree angle; the object above the front of the cupola is the commander's scissors periscope with tubular glare shields installed. *National Archives and Records Administration*

A column of *StuG III Ausf. G*s trek over a muddy road on a desolate plain. At least the first three vehicles have engine starter cranks clamped to the right sides of the upper-rear hull panels. This feature dated to the summer of 1943. The armor skirts on at least the nearest *StuG* are the early type, with a crisscross camouflage pattern of a dark color, green or reddish brown, over the *Dunkelgelb* base color. *National Archives and Records Administration*

The crew of a *StuG III Ausf. G* makes preparations to support the advance of light-infantry troops across a plowed field in the southern part of the Eastern Front. The loader, who is wearing radio headphones, is mounting an MG 34 on the shield. Captured tracks for the Soviet T-34 tank have been put to use as extra armor for the side of the superstructure. A close examination of these tracks, as well as other photos showing the same use of these tracks, reveals that the indentations on the tracks were filled with a hard material, apparently concrete, for additional protection. *National Archives and Records Administration*

Photographed somewhere on the Eastern Front, this *StuG III Ausf. G* bears features that limit its date of production to March 1943. The tubular fender supports were introduced to production in March 1943, while this style of driver's frontal armor, 30 mm of supplemental armor bolted to the stock 50 mm armor, also dates to March 1943. No skirts or skirt brackets are present, which indicates completion before April 1943. A number "2" is painted on the side of the superstructure.
National Archives and Records Administration

On the Eastern Front, a *StuG III Ausf. G* in plain *Dunkelgelb* camouflage paint emerges from a wooded area. On the basis of the style of driver's frontal armor, the presence of tubular fender skirts, and the absence of armored skirts, the month of production of this *StuG* can be established as March 1943. The number "5" is marked on the side of the superstructure. *National Archives and Records Administration*

A whitewashed *StuG III Ausf. G* waits in position while the commander, clad in a white parka, watches the situation to the front. The month of production was between April 1943, when MIAG began installing the early-style skirts, and May 1943, when the smoke grenade launchers were discontinued. These launchers are visible to the sides of the superstructure. Note the dual bogie wheels stowed on the fenders. *National Archives and Records Administration*

Two whitewashed *StuG III Ausf. Gs*, including a vehicle produced by MIAG in April 1943 in the foreground, proceed along a hard-packed roadway in the winter. The *StuG* in the foreground has small, fixed rear mudguards and a Notek taillight or distance indicator, both of which were introduced in February 1943, but the absence of skirts limits this vehicle's production month to no later than April 1943. A whitewashed spare dual bogie wheel is on the rear of the hull, a large storage box is on the engine deck, and spare tracks are in a holder on the side of the superstructure. *Patton Museum*

A *StuG III Ausf. G* of April or May 1943 construction, assigned to a *Heer* (army, as opposed to *Waffen-SS*) unit, exhibits some signs of operational and battle damage. The left mudguard, constructed of sheet metal, has been severely bent, possibly from colliding with an obstacle. The rear spare bogie wheel on the side of the superstructure has taken a hit: a large gouge is on the front side of the rubber tire. Also, the edge of the fender is crumpled, especially toward the rear. *Patton Museum*

The same *StuG III Ausf. G* shown in the preceding photo is viewed from the right side. Although extremely difficult to see, manipulation of the photograph reveals that a tactical sign for a *Sturmgeschütz* unit with an illegible three-digit number inside it is on the right side of the front plate of the glacis, while a number, apparently the chassis number, is painted in white on the left side of that plate. Note the crumpled mudguard and the damage to the rear portion of the front smoke grenade launcher tube. *Patton Museum*

The classic MIAG pattern of *Zimmerit* is seen to excellent effect in this photo of a *StuG III Ausf. G*. The *Zimmerit* extended to the fronts of the mudguards on this vehicle. Tubular glare shields are attached to the objectives of the commander's scissors periscope. On the right side of the vehicle, the second panel of the skirt is missing and the mounting rail is twisted. A section of spare track offered a bit of extra protection to the front of the "shoulder" of the superstructure. It is likely this vehicle was produced between September and December 1943: it features the *Zimmerit* that MIAG introduced in September but lacks the shot deflector for the cupola, which MIAG began installing in December 1943. *Patton Museum*

Crewmen are preparing a *StuG III Ausf. G* for service while a small dog sitting on the cupola hatch observes the proceedings. The vehicle exhibits MIAG-type *Zimmerit*, and camouflage paint has been applied over the *Dunkelgelb* base color in the form of a dark color with an even-darker color as a border. A clear view is available of the plugged socket for attaching a hubcap to the sprocket; these plugs had a slot in the center. The rear skirt panel has been cut narrower in width. The mantlet, fabricated from screwed plates, was the type with an opening at the upper left for a coaxial machine gun, introduced to the MIAG assembly line in May 1944. Early-type skirts and brackets are present: while this style of skirt was mostly phased out by the end of February 1944, it was still installed on some *StuG III Ausf. G*s through June of that year. This vehicle was likely built in or around May 1944. *Patton Museum*

A column of *StuG III Ausf. G*s advance. Each vehicle has a cover over the mantlet and the front end of the superstructure. Early-model skirts are installed on the vehicle to the front. The presence of these skirts and the absence of *Zimmerit* indicate a production timeframe of sometime between April and August 1943. The commander has turned his revolving cupola so the hatch is on the right side. This type of cupola was installed on MIAG vehicles from February to November 1943. *Patton Museum*

Sturmgeschütz crews are conferring or relaxing during a pause in a road march. A black-and-white *Balkenkreuz* identification cross is on the skirt, which is the late type with triangular holders. The mantlet is the early type, fabricated from armor plates screwed together. Supplemental armor is bolted to the bow. *Patton Museum*

The Deutsches Panzermuseum, Munster, Germany, preserves this *StuG III Ausf. G*. It features the cast mantlet with opening for coaxial machine gun, as manufactured by Alkett from September 1944 to the end of production. Other features include the driver's frontal armor secured with eight hex nuts, the shot deflector to the front of the cupola, and 80 mm welded frontal armor on the bow. On the bow is the insignia of *Sturmgeschütz*brigade 191. *Massimo Foti*

At the center of the bow is the Notek blackout headlight. No other headlights are present. The muzzle brake on the 7.5 cm L/48 gun is the type with two chambers and two large, circular blast faces, used on *StuG III*s made by Alkett and MIAG from June 1944 to the end of production. *Massimo Foti*

The late-type cast mantlet is viewed from the right side, showing the moderately rough texture of the surface. Several large gouges are on the side of the mantlet. The inspection hatches on the bow have the two-panel doors with interior-mounted hinges. Between the inboard hinges of the left hatch is a stop for the inboard door. *Massimo Foti*

The frontal plate of the driver's compartment is viewed close-up. Eight hex nuts secure it in place: five on the top and three on the bottom. The driver's armored visor is recessed in the frontal plate. On the bow deck to the front of the visor is a shot deflector, designed to prevent projectiles ricocheting off the deck from penetrating the front of the driver's compartment. A section of two spare track links is stored above the driver's compartment. *Massimo Foti*

The late-type cast mantlet has a port near the upper corner for a coaxial MG 34 7.92 mm machine gun. *Massimo Foti*

The sprockets on the Munster *StuG III Ausf. G* are a late type with the hubcap eliminated, and with a small hole at the center of the hub for mounting on a lathe during production. The sprocket is mounted to the final drive with twenty lug nuts. *Massimo Foti*

The two forward sets of bogie wheels on the left side of the vehicle are depicted. Some of the outer portion of the rubber tire on the top of the front wheel has broken off. This pattern of bogie wheel remained standard throughout most of the production runs of the various models of the *StuG III* except for the first production batch of the *Ausf. A. Massimo Foti*

The track support rollers on this *StuG III Ausf. G* are the late-production type: all steel, with six lightening holes and no spokes. Between the roller and the sprocket is the front shock absorber. *Massimo Foti*

The cast mantlet is viewed from the upper left, showing the position of the port for the coaxial MG 34. This type of mantlet also was referred to as the *Saukopfblende* or *Topfblende. Massimo Foti*

The superstructure roof is seen from the front left. The raised hex-head screws that fasten the roof to the superstructure replaced slotted, countersunk screws from May 1944 to the end of production. At the front corners of the roof and at the center of the roof to the right of the cupola are mounting points, called *Pilze*, for a two-ton auxiliary jib boom. This vehicle also had *Pilze* on the rear corners of the roof, for a total of five *Pilze*. The early configuration of *Pilze* on the *StuG III Ausf. G* had only three of them. Near the front right corner of the roof is the top plate of the *Nahverteidigunswaffe* close-in defense weapon, to the rear of which is the mount for the late-type, remote-controlled machine gun installation. *Massimo Foti*

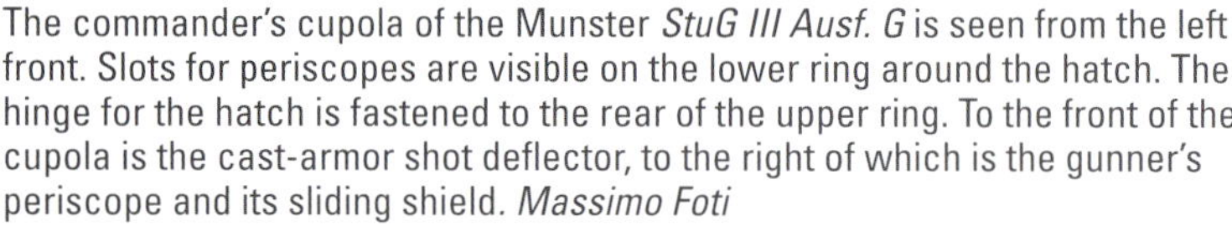

The commander's cupola of the Munster *StuG III Ausf. G* is seen from the left front. Slots for periscopes are visible on the lower ring around the hatch. The hinge for the hatch is fastened to the rear of the upper ring. To the front of the cupola is the cast-armor shot deflector, to the right of which is the gunner's periscope and its sliding shield. *Massimo Foti*

The superstructure is viewed from its left rear corner. On the left rear of the superstructure is a radio antenna with a brown insulator at its base. This antenna was for the Fu 15 radio receiver and Fu 16 transmitter. To the far right, on the rear of the superstructure, is a ventilator cover. *Massimo Foti*

The engine deck of the *StuG III Ausf. G* is viewed from the left rear corner of the superstructure roof, providing a detailed view of the engine maintenance hatches and the ventilator covers mounted on them. In the foreground is a radio antenna. A rack made of metal straps is attached to the engine deck, for retaining baggage and stored gear, such as the two Jerry cans seen here. A bogie wheel assembly is on each rear corner of the deck. *Massimo Foti*

The Munster *StuG III Ausf. G* is seen from the right rear. At the rear of the hull is the right idler. This was the second and final pattern of idler used on the *StuG III*s, and it entered production with the *Ausf. C* at Alkett in March 1941. *Massimo Foti*

Details of the rear of the superstructure are displayed, including the two radio antenna mounts and the ventilator cover on the rear plate of the superstructure, and the lifting ring welded at an angle to the side of the superstructure. A lifting hook is on the side of the engine compartment, directly below the right antenna mount. *Massimo Foti*

The superstructure roof is seen from the right side, with the focus on the mount for the remote-controlled machine gun, directly to the front of the loader's hatch, and, in the center foreground, the top plate of the *Nahverteidigunswaffe* close-in defense weapon. The *Nahverteidigunswaffe* was a fully rotating launcher of 92 mm diameter that fired smoke bombs or antipersonnel grenades. The launcher was mounted to the bottom of the round plate seen here. Note also the dust cover between the mantlet and the superstructure to the lower right. *Massimo Foti*

Stored on the right fender are a shovel, an axe, and a jack. On the turret roof a few inches to the front of the right antenna is the right rear mount for installing an auxiliary jib boom, an accessory that made it much more convenient to lift heavy objects, such as the engine, for repairs in the field. *Massimo Foti*

In a wider view from the right front of the superstructure, details of the weld beads on the structural armor are in view. On the upper inside of the numeral "0" is a large gouge, apparently inflicted by a projectile that failed to penetrate the armor. *Massimo Foti*

The *StuG III Ausf. G* at Munster is viewed from the right front. The fenders on this vehicle have an odd antiskid tread pattern not encountered in wartime photos of German or Finnish *StuG III*s, so they are possibly postwar additions. *Massimo Foti*

CHAPTER 4
Sturmhaubitze

Based on the Alkett *StuG III Ausf. G* chassis, the *Sturmhaubitze 42* (*StuH 42*) featured a version of the 10.5 cm leFH 18 howitzer and was designed to provide highly mobile infantry support with a direct- or indirect-fire capability. In this photo of two *StuH 42*s moving along a forest road, the lead vehicle has Alkett's factory-applied waffle-pattern *Zimmerit* and late-model armor skirts. The *StuH 42*s employed both cast mantlets, as seen here, and mantlets assembled from screwed-together armor plate. *SA-Kuva*

As the *Sturmgeschütz* was being employed more and more as an antitank gun, the infantry was left without their own assault gun, the role for which the *Sturmgeschütz* had originally been intended. This led to the creation of the pilot model of a new vehicle, the *Sturmhaubitze*, which is described in Volume 1 in this series. Armed with the potent 10.5 cm *Sturmhaubitze*, the prototype was well-received by Hitler and the military alike, and an initial production group of twelve were produced, based on rebuilt *Sturmgeschütz*. Nine of these were issued to *3.Batterie* of *Sturmgeschütz-Abteilung 185* for use near Leningrad.

The converted vehicles were followed by series production, which began at Alkett in March 1943. While the prototype had been created from a *Sturmgeschütz Ausf. F/8*, the series production vehicles were based on the *Sturmgeschütz Ausf. G*. Installing the light field howitzer in the vehicle did require some changes to the vehicle, including notably the installation of different ammunition racks.

The *Sturmhaubitze*, or *StuH*, was produced exclusively by Alkett, and its production was intermingled with that of the *StuG Ausf. G*. In fact, the chassis, or *fahrgestell*, numbers of the two types were intermingled, which along with the Russian capture of the Alkett plant makes it difficult to pinpoint the exact number of *Sturmhaubitze* produced. However, the number of *Sturmhaubitze* can be reliably put at approximately 1,300 vehicles. Their chassis numbers were in the range of 92151 to 108920. *Sturmhaubitze* production spanned March 1943 until April 1945.

A *StuH 42* heavily laden with troops pauses while advancing through tall grass. A spare dual bogie wheel is visible on the far side of the 10.5 cm howitzer barrel. The muzzle brake is the leFH 18/40 type. Alkett-style *Zimmerit* is in evidence on the superstructure. The armored skirts are modified, coming up only to a little above the fenders; above that armor, a piece of skirt has been laid against the superstructure for a little extra protection. *Patton Museum*

A *StuH 42* is first in line next to several *StuG III*s. A very dark-colored muzzle cover and mantlet/superstructure cover are in place. Note how the latter cover extends to the rear of the superstructure roof. *Patton Museum*

Crewmen carry 10.5 cm shells to a *StuH 42*. The 10.5 cm leFH 18 howitzer fired separate shells and propellant cartridges. The *StuH 42* had a capacity for carrying thirty-six rounds of 10.5 cm ammunition. A rack is on the engine deck for holding baggage and equipment, and the jack is visible toward the rear of the fender. *National Archives and Records Administration*

The same vehicle as the one in the preceding photo is viewed close-up as crewmen pass 10.5 cm shells from the stack on the fender of the *StuH 42* up to the soldier in the loader's hatch. By mid-1943, fixed ammunition, with the shell mated to the cartridge, was available for use for the *StuH 42*s. *National Archives and Records Administration*

Sturmhaubitze	
Make	Alkett
Quantity	approx. 1,300
Dimensions	
Length	20′ 13/4″
Width	9′ 7″
Height	7′ 3/4″
Weight	23.9 tons
Performance	
Maximum speed	25 mph
Cruising speed	12.5 mph
Cross-country	6 mph
Range, on road	99 miles
Range, cross-country	62 miles
Trench crossing	7.5′
Crew	4
Communications	Fu 16 or Fu.15
Armament	
Weapon, main	10.5 cm *StuH* 42
Secondary	2 x 7.92 mm MG 34
Elevation	-6 to +20 degrees
Traverse	10 degrees right; 10 degrees left
Ammo stowage, main	36 rounds
7.92 mm	600 rounds
Automotive	
Engine make	Maybach
Engine model	HL 120 TRM
Engine configuration	V-12, liquid cooled
Engine displacement	11.9 liters
Engine horsepower	265 @ 2,600 rpm
Fuel capacity	82 gallons
Transmission	SSG 77
Speeds	6 + reverse
Steering	differential
Track	Kgs 61/400/120
Links per side	93

A *StuH 42* with abundant local camouflage hanging from the vehicle rounds a street corner in a town en route to the front. A light-colored dust cover is over the muzzle brake of the 10.5 cm howitzer. A rack on the engine deck helps keep the baggage and equipment from sliding off. This gear includes a large storage box. Several spare dual bogie wheels are stashed between the armored skirt and the hull. *National Archives and Records Administration*

Infantry troops, including some foreign auxiliaries, are piling aboard a *StuH 42* on the Eastern Front. This vehicle features low-cut skirts and thin, supplemental armor leaning against the superstructure sides. A *Balkenkreuz* and the number "133" are painted on the supplemental armor and the rear of the hull. A retainer for equipment made of two boards with three mounting brackets has been installed on the rear of the engine deck as a modification. *National Archives and Records Administration*

A *StuH 42* of April or May 1943 production is viewed from the left side. This vehicle has the mantlet fabricated from armor plates. The smoke grenade launchers were discontinued in May 1943. The *StuH 42* is distinguishable from the *StuG III Ausf. G* by the former's thicker and shorter howitzer barrel and larger muzzle brake. *Patton Museum*

This *StuH 42*, displayed in the immediate post-World War II years at Aberdeen Proving Ground, is a very late production (January 1945 or later) vehicle with no muzzle brake (deleted beginning in September 1944), cannon travel lock (introduced July 1944), rotating MG 34 mount introduced (introduced July 1944), rotating cupola (introduced September 1944), and the extended hull side plated with redesigned lifting lugs (introduced January 1945). The screwed mantlet fitted to this *StuH* is an anomaly; by this date, it should have had a coaxial machine gun mount. *Patton Museum*

Alkett used available *StuG III Ausf. G* chassis when assembling the *StuH 42*s. The bow of this example has the 80 mm integral armor introduced at Alkett in April 1943. The front one-third of the left fender has been wracked, and the right mudguard is missing. The cupola lacks a shot deflector, and the driver's supplemental armor is attached with eight hex screws: five along the top edge and three at the bottom. *Patton Museum*

CHAPTER 5
Sturmgeschütz IV

This is one of the first thirty *StuG IV*s completed at Krupp-Grusonwerk in Magdeberg, Germany, in December 1943. These vehicles constituted modified *StuG III Ausf. G* superstructures on *PzKpfw IV* chassis. The *Zimmerit* on the frontal armor of the driver's compartment is applied in neat columns of horizontal ridges, with grids scratched into the surface of the *Zimmerit*. On the other surfaces, the *Zimmerit* is applied largely in zigzag patterns. The *Zimmerit* on each mudguard has a cross shape scratched into it, dividing the *Zimmerit* into four rectangular grids. *Patton Museum*

The concept of a *Sturmgeschütz* based on the *Panzerkampfwagen IV* chassis was first presented by Krupp in 1943. That design, Krupp drawing number W1468 of February 1943, utilized the *Sturmgeschütz Ausf. F* superstructure on the proposed *Panzer IV* chassis 9./B. W., rather than the 8./B.W. then in production. The proposed *Sturmgeschütz IV* design, projected to weigh 28.26 tons, was rejected largely due to the weight, which was substantially heavier than a *Sturmgeschütz III*. Thus, the project was abandoned the same month it began.

Planning for a *Sturmgeschütz* based on the *Panzerkampfwagen IV* chassis resumed in December 1943. This was the result of a November 26, 1943, Allied bomb raid on Alkett, which saw over 1,400 tons of bombs, both high explosive and incendiary, target the plant with considerable effect. Alkett *Sturmgeschütz III* production fell from 255 units in October to twenty-four in December, and the plant was subjected to bombing again, twice in January 1944.

Faced with a critical shortage of the increasingly important *Sturmgeschütz*, at a conference in early December 1943 the decision was made to mount a *Sturmgeschütz III Ausf. G* superstructure on a Krupp *Panzer IV* 7./B.W. chassis.

These two major components could be mated with a relatively minimal modification. Specifically, a driver's compartment had to be fabricated and added to the front left side of the superstructure, and a plate was made to fill the gap between the transmission cover and the leading edge of the *Sturmgeschütz* superstructure. Hitler was shown the prototype in mid-December 1943 and approved the project.

Because of the increasing deficit in *Sturmgeschütz III* production, Krupp Grusonwerk was asked to place the new vehicle in production quickly. Accordingly, thirty of the vehicles were completed in December 1943, and by the time the war ended, 1,141 had been produced.

As the production of the *Panzerkampfwagen IV Ausf. H*, on which the *Sturmgeschütz IV* was initially based, was phased out in favor of the *Panzerkampfwagen IV Ausf. J*, these chassis began to be used for the *Sturmgeschütz IV* as well. Among the changes made to the chassis during the production run were the reduction of return rollers from four per side to three per side, forming the tow brackets integral with the hull sides, converting to flame-arresting mufflers, and adding brackets for use with tow bars to the rear of the hull.

The *Sturmgeschütz IV* superstructure underwent the same evolution as did *Sturmgeschütz III Ausf. G* superstructure, which was being produced concurrently.

Most of the *Sturmgeschütz IV* were used to equip single *Sturmgeschütz* companies attached to infantry divisions. As such, the vehicles were found both on the Eastern and Western Fronts.

Sturmgeschütz IV	
Make	Krupp Grusonwerk
Chassis (Fgst) number	89324–89382 (converted using Nibelungenwerk chassis), 100001–101111 (Krupp chassis)
Quantity	1,141
Dimensions	
Length	21′ 113/4″
Width	9′ 7″
Height	7′ 5/8″
Weight	25.9 tons
Performance	
Maximum speed	24 mph
Cruising speed	12.5 mph
Cross-country	6 mph
Range, on road	99 miles
Range, cross-country	62 miles
Trench crossing	7.5′
Crew	4
Communications	transmitter and receiver
Armament	
Weapon, main	7.5 cm *StuK* L/40
Secondary	1 x 7.92 mm MG 34
Elevation	-6 to +20 degrees
Traverse	10 degrees right; 10 degrees left
Ammo stowage, main	61 rounds
7.92 mm	600 rounds
Automotive	
Engine make	Maybach
Engine model	HL 120 TRM
Engine configuration	V-12, liquid cooled
Engine displacement	11.9 liters
Engine horsepower	265 @ 2,600 rpm
Fuel capacity	82 gallons
Transmission	SSG 76
Speeds	6 + reverse
Steering	differential
Track	Kgs 61/400/120
Links per side	99

In a factory, *StuG IV*s are undergoing construction. On the line to the left are nine vehicles with the main guns and the superstructure roofs still to be installed. To the side of this are coils of track assemblies and 75 mm guns and their mounts. To the right are three *StuG IV*s with the main guns and the roofs installed. Muzzle brakes are not yet installed on the guns. *Patton Museum*

The *Zimmerit* antimagnetic paste on this *StuG IV*, possibly the same one seen in the photo on page 106, is particularly interesting. It is not applied in a uniform manner but is rather haphazard, with varying sizes of grids, different orientations of the ridges, and widely dissimilar sizes of the ridges. *Zimmerit* has also been applied to the tops and sides of the track guards and to the lower hull. Details of the hangers for the *Schürzen* also are in view. The patterns and contours of the *Zimmerit* on the rear side of the same *StuG IV* are apparent in this factory photo. Six spare track links are stored in holders on the side of the superstructure. *Patton Museum*

2

A late-production *StuG IV* completed in August or September 1944 features a *Hinterhalt-Tarnung* (ambush camouflage) scheme, particularly noticeable on the *Schürzen*. This scheme incorporated patterns of *Rotbraun* (reddish brown) and *Olivgrün* (olive green) over the *Dunkelgelb* (dark yellow) base color, with small dabs of *Dunkelgelb* on the darker patterns to simulate the effect of daylight through foliage. Mounted on the roof is a *Rundumfeuer* (all-around fire) remote-controlled machine gun mount. *Patton Museum*

A column of *StuG IVs* is paused on a street or dock in Greece in 1944. Another photo exists of a group of similarly painted *StuG IVs* in Thessaloniki, Greece, in 1944, so this photo may have been taken there at the same time as well. The vehicles all are painted in *Dunkelgelb* without additional camouflage paint. The second vehicle has an angled splash guard on the frontal plate above and to the rear of the driver's compartment. *Patton Museum*

General Field Marshal Albert Kesselring, in the light-colored coat, is viewing a firing demonstration of a *StuG IV* in the mountains of Italy in 1944. A fabric cover is installed over the mantlet, and concrete has been added to the front of the driver's frontal armor for added protection. This was accomplished by placing a wooden form to the front of the compartment and packing it with mixed concrete.
Patton Museum

The same *StuG IV* with Kesselring aboard is seen from a closer perspective. On the left fender is a Bosch headlight. The gunner's periscopic sight is protruding through the superstructure roof. *Patton Museum*

Kesselring, right, watches a *StuG IV* during a firing demonstration in Italy in 1944. Brush had been piled up on the fenders for an additional degree of camouflage. *Bundesarchiv*

The tactical number "331" is on one of the skirt sections on this *StuG IV*, and a black-and-white *Balkenkreuz* is below the number. Spare tracks are on the bow and the glacis, and more spare track links have been arranged around the driver's compartment. *Patton Museum*

A *StuG IV* is parked next to a Soviet SU-85 tank destroyer on the Eastern Front. Two unditching beams made of logs are resting in special racks on the rear of the hull. An evergreen tree has been wedged into the space next to the right *Schürzen* for camouflage. The rear panel of the skirt is missing.
National Archives and Records Administration

The brake access doors of this *StuG IV* are open, as is the driver's hatch door, which was hinged on the left side. There is a fabric cover installed over the mantlet of the 7.5 cm gun, and camouflage material—brush or netting or perhaps both—is draped over the main gun and the superstructure. Spare track links and sections are lying in a jumble on the glacis. *Patton Museum*

A soldier observes the effect of the fire of two *StuG IVs* in a clearing. The vehicle to the right appears to have simply a base color of Dunkelgelb without any additional camouflage colors. *SA-Kuva*

During the advance of Canadian forces to Pontecorvo, Italy, they knocked out this *StuG IV*. The photograph was taken on May 26, 1944. The explosion that destroyed the vehicle tore up the front end and blew off the superstructure roof and the main gun, which is lying upside down in the foreground. Note the irregular contours of the *Zimmerit* on the side of the superstructure.
National Archives and Records Administration

A group of GIs inspect a captured *StuG IV* jammed in a narrow lane in hedgerow country. Lying upside down on the mantlet is a toolbox. Lying on the right side of the glacis is a C-shaped tow hook. The muzzle of the 7.5 cm gun has the so-called "oval" shape. *National Archives and Records Administration*

British soldiers are inspecting a group of captured German and Italian vehicles in Italy in the summer of 1944. In the foreground is a *StuG IV*, followed to the rear by a *StuG III Ausf. G*, a badly shot-up *Marder II*, an equally shot-riddled *Marder III Ausf. H*, and two Italian Semovente M40-75/18 self-propelled guns. To the front of the machine gun shield on the *StuG IV* is a hinged cover for the mantlet, folded back. *Patton Museum*

A British Tommy is scrutinizing a captured *StuG IV* adjacent to a camouflaged gun position, likely in Italy. It appears that concrete "armor" has been added to the front and side of the driver's compartment: note the curved side along that compartment, which is consistent with add-on concrete reinforcing. Spare tracks have been added to the superstructure for extra protection, and the plate in front of the right side of the superstructure may have been part of the effort to beef-up the protection. *Patton Museum*

British soldiers are investigating a captured *StuG IV*; judging by their uniforms and the surroundings, the photo probably was taken in Italy. This vehicle has the hinged cover over the mantlet. The crew had placed a large storage box on the right fender and another one on the rear deck. The left *Schürzen* hanger has been destroyed, and several of the plates are missing. Note the camouflage pattern on the remaining plates. *Patton Museum*

A GI inspects the remains of a *StuG IV* at Periers, France, on July 24, 1944. The *Schürzen* hanger is twisted wreckage. The vehicle's jack is lying against the sprocket. The rubber tires were burned off several of the bogie wheels. Several spare track links are stored on the upper part of the side of the superstructure. *National Archives and Records Administration*

A *StuG IV* is seen at close range, with a fairly good view of the hinged cover over the mantlet. Although it is not easily discerned in this photo, the spare track section on the vertical part of the bow was not simply resting in the bracket: two bolts inserted through openings in track guide horns and threaded through retainers acted to hold the track in place. *Patton Museum*

The front of the driver's compartment and other features on the superstructure of a *StuG IV* are viewed from above the left side of the glacis. The bulge to the front of the driver's frontal armor is a ventilation scoop, with the opening facing to the rear. On top of the driver's compartment, to the front of the hatch, are two periscope hoods; they are fitted with bolt-on shields to protect the periscopes from rain and glare. *Patton Museum*

The same *StuG IV* is viewed from the left side, showing the exterior of the driver's hatch door. The door has a grab handle and two stops welded to the outer edge. The left periscope hood is seen from the side. Two short sections of spare track links are leaning against the driver's compartment. *Patton Museum*

The cupola of a *StuG IV* is seen from the rear. The cupola hatch door had a hinged panel with a grab handle; this panel allowed the commander to deploy his scissors periscope without opening the entire hatch door. *Patton Museum*

The barrel was blown off this *StuG IV* nearly flush with the front of the mantlet. The blast that devastated the front end of this vehicle also seems to have blown off much of the *Zimmerit* from the glacis. Concrete has been added to the front of the superstructure for enhanced protection from frontal fire. The mantlet cover lacks the turned-down outer edges frequently seen on these covers. *Patton Museum*

The superstructure roof has been blown off this *StuG IV*, revealing the breech end of the 7.5 cm gun and its recoil and recuperator cylinders to the left, and one of the 7.5 cm ammunition bins to the right. This bin held eight rounds, and the front end of the box extended into an opening into the right front of the superstructure. More ammunition was stored below this bin. A spare bogie wheel set is on the side of the superstructure. *National Archives and Records Administration*

A late-production *StuG IV* with a full set of *Schürzen* is displayed. On the superstructure roof to the front of the loader's hatch is a *Rundumfeuer* (all-around fire) remote-controlled MG 34 machine gun mount and shield. Although the original photograph is grainy, there appears to be a rough coat of *Zimmerit* on the hull, mudguards, and superstructure, without a discernible texture or pattern. Note the two short posts with angled tops on the driver's compartment; these were stops for holding the hatch door open. *National Archives and Records Administration*